IMAGES OF ENGLAND

NORBURY, THORNTON HEATH AND BROAD GREEN

Dear Richard, Tom
Johnny

With All My Love
Michael (GRANDAD)

Thornton Heath Clock Tower illuminated for the Coronation of King George VI, 1937.

IMAGES OF ENGLAND

NORBURY, THORNTON HEATH AND BROAD GREEN

RAYMOND WHEELER

The
History
Press

A typical horse-drawn van of the Edwardian period, owned by G. Willis of Sumner Road, Broad Green.

First published 2000
Reprinted 2003

Reprinted in 2014 by
The History Press
The Mill, Brimscombe Port,
Stroud, Gloucestershire, GL5 2QG
www.thehistorypress.co.uk

© Raymond Wheeler, 2000, 2014

The right of Raymond Wheeler to be identified as the Author of this work has been asserted in accordance with the Copyrights, Designs and Patents Act 1988.

British Library Cataloguing in Publication Data.
A catalogue record for this book is available from the British Library.

ISBN 978 0 7524 2164 3

Printed and bound in Great Britain by
Marston Book Services Limited, Oxfordshire

Contents

Acknowledgements

The pictures appearing in this book have come from various sources and collections, including my own. I am grateful to the following people and organizations, who have lent them or given me permission for their pictures to be reproduced:

P.J. Davies; Dennis Finch; John Gent; Mrs Law; Arthur Moyles; *Croydon Advertiser*; Christine Evans, Tom Ross and Paul Wenham of St Stephen's, Norbury and Thornton Heath; Mrs Mary Shelton-Smith, head teacher of Winterbourne Girls' School.

The following photographs have come from the collection belonging to the Croydon Local Studies Library ('a' denotes top picture, 'b' bottom picture): Page 4, 9, 11a, 18ab, 22a, 24b, 27b, 31, 36, 43a, 44a, 45ab, 46, 47ab, 48ab, 49, 51ab, 54ab, 57ab, 58, 59a, 60ab, 61b, 62b, 63b, 64b, 65, 67, 68ab, 69, 70ab, 71, 72, 73, 74ab, 76b, 79, 85b, 88b, 89a, 91, 92ab, 93b, 96a, 98, 99ab, 101, 106b, 107, 109b, 110a, 117a, 118ab, 119, 120, 121, 122.

I am also extremely grateful for the support of the many people who have contributed in one way or another in the production of this book. I would particularly like to mention Steve Roud, Steve Griffiths, Christine Corner, Christine Smith and all the staff at Croydon Local Studies Library for their support and use of facilities; Gerry Coll for his encouragement; Revd John Clevely and Sheila Buckner of Beulah Family Church; Alan Turner; Jack Saunders; and Peter Davies of Canada. Finally a big thank-you to my wife, Susan, for her support throughout and to my children, Ruth and Peter, for their tolerance and support at having to put up with days spent hogging the computer, at the library or when nothing seemed to go right!

Introduction

Very little has been published on Norbury, Thornton Heath or Broad Green. It was partly to remedy this and to share something of my place of origin that this pictorial history was put together.

Thornton Heath lies in the valley of the Norbury Brook (which becomes the River Graveney beyond Hermitage Bridge), while the highest point is Pollards Hill at 212ft above sea level. The ancient Manor of Croydon was divided into sub-manors and so Norbury gets its name from the North Borough or North Bury. As its name implies, there was a heath at Thornton Heath. A valuation of the Manor of Norbury in the year 1266 stated that the heath was capable of feeding 500 sheep. Broad Green, also, was an open space: a triangular green at the western extremity of Croydon Common.

Lonely Thornton Heath with its open spaces and nearness to the Norwood Hills provided an ambush point for highway robbers. Early maps marked Thornton Heath as Gallows Green and the Croydon parish registers record the execution of several criminals during the eighteenth century. The gibbet is supposed to have stood opposite where the bingo hall is now.

From 1337 to 1857 the old Manor of Norbury was in the possession of the Carew family of Beddington. The manor house was situated on the corner of Kensington Avenue and Norbury Avenue. In later years it was known as Norbury Farm. One of the tenants, William Coles, built Norbury Hall, now an old people's home with the grounds a public park off Craignish Avenue. To the south lay the manor of Bensham or Whitehorse.

Until the late nineteenth century Norbury and Thornton Heath was still open country, with several remnants of ancient oak woodland, as maps and estate plans will testify. Farms existed at Parchmore, Biggin, Waddon Marsh, Norbury and Colliers Water. In 1894 cuckoos, linnets, skylarks and nightingales were recorded, and the smell of lavender and peppermint pervaded the air. Old lanes included Green Lane, Bensham Lane across the common fields, Waddon Marsh Lane, and Colliers Water Lane (a reminder of the charcoal-burning industry of the Great North Wood), winding its way to join Green Lane and Whitehorse Lane. Other lanes led up the slope to Upper Norwood and the Beulah Spa. A large pond existed on the heath, no doubt to water the livestock grazing there. After enclosure in 1800 a hamlet developed around the pond and towards the end of the century a fountain was installed to commemorate Queen Victoria's Golden Jubilee. In 1818 it was reckoned there were only seventy-eight houses in Thornton Heath.

Some larger mansions had been built in the early nineteenth century but the coming of the railway to Thornton Heath in 1862 made it possible for prosperous merchants and clerks from

London to reside there. Villas sprang up along the London Road and Brigstock Road (as Colliers Water Lane was later renamed). New houses and cottages were built around the Beulah Road area in close proximity to the railway station. The district was named New Thornton Heath to distinguish it from the original hamlet around the Pond. The area west of the London Road around Sumner Road, as well as the Whitehorse Road district, also began to grow as Croydon expanded northwards. A new private development came about in North Park (Croydon Lodge estate).

The biggest explosion of development took place during the period 1890 to 1914 as the large villa estates from the early nineteenth century were sold off for development prior to the First World War. Lured by advertisements extolling the delights of fresh air and countryside, new-comers were drawn to the new housing springing up all round. Alongside new housing came schools, libraries, churches, bandstands, sports facilities and dance halls, then cinemas. As a fine mark of civic pride Thornton Heath Clock Tower was erected in 1900 to commemorate the new century and acknowledging the importance of the area now known as the 'High Street' as a commercial centre.

Norbury also began to grow, but later than Broad Green or Thornton Heath. There was still much green space at the time of the First World War. Norbury could even boast four golf courses and Pollards Hill was advertised as a garden village. Open farmland still existed after the First World War to the east of the railway line along Green Lane and the Ingram Estate. However, by 1930 most of the road pattern we know today in north-west Croydon was complete.

This book takes the form of a journey back in time reflecting on the remarkable growth of north-west Croydon. The journey begins at Norbury, then travels down the London Road past the Pond to the Broad Green district. After returning to the Pond, we have a look at West Thornton, then move along Brigstock Road to the High Street and the Whitehorse area. The journey finishes in New Thornton Heath. There follows a brief glimpse of the war years and finally some recently discovered photographs of the construction of St Stephen's church, a parish that grew out of a church in Broad Green and which encompasses both a part of Thornton Heath and of Norbury.

A number of the photographs featured in this book have been seen before in other books on Croydon but the opportunity has been taken to bring these together to present them in the context of the local area. Many others are new and unpublished and I trust will provide further insights into the history of Norbury, Thornton Heath and Broad Green. In view of the size of the area covered some parts have not been depicted but this collection has been put together on the basis of photographs available to the author. Deliberately, I have not included any photographs of Crystal Palace Football Club as its history has been covered in a separate volume published by The History Press. Above all, I hope that this selection will provide readers with a glimpse into the social, economic and geographic history of this part of north-west Croydon.

In conclusion, the area has seen many population changes. With the advent of the railways it became, and is still, a major commuter area. It is a mixed community; a community that still works, worships and plays. It is to the people of this area of Croydon, the area where I grew up, that this book is dedicated.

Raymond Wheeler
2000

One

Norbury

Norbury Manor Farm, seen here around 1905, was the ancient manor house for the estate of Norbury, which until 1859 was in the possession of the Carew family. It stood approximately where Kensington Avenue and Norbury Avenue meet. The farmhouse and buildings were demolished in 1914.

The tram is standing on Hermitage Bridge which crossed the River Graveney. At this point the stream formed the boundary between the ancient parishes of Croydon and Streatham and after the formation of the London County Council it became the boundary between the County Borough of Croydon and the Metropolitan Borough of Wandsworth. A Roman ford was discovered here in the 1960s.

The terminus of Croydon Corporation's tram route from Purley to Norbury, which opened on 25 September 1901, at Hermitage Bridge. The LCC extended their Streatham route here in 1909 but passengers had to change tramcars. The six-inch gap between the two authorities' lines was not filled until 1926, enabling through running to take place between Embankment and Purley. Here Bank Holiday crowds are waiting for the tram to take them to the open countryside around Purley. On the left is the site of the later police station, built in 1925.

The extension of the LCC tram route to Norbury in 1909 brought additional traffic to both tramway systems by passengers wanting to make the through journey to/from London. To cater for the increased traffic Croydon laid in new crossovers in that year.

Norbury station opened in 1878 with only two wooden platforms. When the line from East Croydon to Balham was widened to four tracks in 1903 the station was rebuilt along with others on the same stretch of line. An up Eastbourne express is passing through in this photograph.

Many of the shopping parades of Norbury were built during the first decade of the twentieth century. Norbury Parade was erected in 1901. Chesterton and Sons, whose Norbury estate office is here seen on the left, were responsible for the sale of much of the building land around Norbury. The General Motor Car Company served the needs of the Edwardian motorist.

Much of the western side of the London Road consisted of private houses. In the 1920s shop units were built in the front gardens as the importance of Norbury as a commercial centre increased. On the right is Victoria Parade, built in 1903 to the design of C. Spencer.

A trade postcard of a Norbury shop window devoted completely to an advertisement display for Sandows Cocoa.

St Helen's Road and St Helen's Crescent were the first developments in Norbury. Large detached villas were constructed on the corner with London Road 1886, together with these semi-detached properties opposite the triangle. The remaining houses, a number in the Arts and Crafts style, were built around 1900. The chestnut trees of the central green had not been planted in this view of 1905.

Near the corner of Stanford Road, with the South Suburban Co-operative Society's store on the right, c. 1930. The shop premises are still a supermarket.

On 14 June 1914 a ferocious storm hit parts of south London with thunder, lightning and torrential rain for about three hours causing flooding throughout the area. For a while even the tram service was suspended. Spectators are standing near the corner of Northborough Road watching carefully the progress of the bus through the flooded street.

King Edward VII's Parade. The glass canopy over the pavement is outside the King Edward Hall, one-time social venue of Norbury. Over the years it was home to the first Baptist congregation, a skating rink and, as seen in this photograph, the Norbury cinema from 1911 to 1937 until competition from the Rex cinema forced it to close. After the Second World War it became the paint warehouse of Walter Carson & Sons Ltd. The building is now a furniture store.

The Rex cinema, part of the ABC circuit, was much loved in Norbury. Opened on Monday 4 January 1937 by Lt Colonel Glyn Mason, Member of Parliament for Croydon North, the Rex had a strikingly modern interior. The architect was Douglas Harrington. The first films shown were the Fred Astaire-Ginger Rogers musical *Swing Time* and Jack Haley in *Mr Cinderella*. The Rex finally closed on Saturday 17 February 1962 and was later demolished. The office block, Radnor House, was built on the site which has been converted into apartments.

Semley Road, 1911. At this time the Baptist church had not been built and the hill in the distance, land 'ripe for development', would later be covered with houses. Lady Stanford of Preston Park, Brighton, owned much of this area and many of the later roads were named after Wiltshire villages where her first husband originated.

The Housing Act of 1900 allowed councils to build houses on land outside their boundaries. The first area to be acquired by the London County Council under the Act was the 30-acre Norbury Estate, bought for £18,000 in 1901. The aim was to build simple, dignified cottages with each one being given as attractive an outlook as possible. The architectural style included many details inspired by the Arts and Crafts movement.

With a background of Norbury Hall, W.G. Grace is batting against Australia in 1888. He had been enlisted to play for G.I. Thornton's XI. Norbury Hall had been purchased by James W. Hobbs, a Croydon builder and owner of a joinery works off Morland Road. He became Croydon's second mayor but was imprisoned for twelve years in 1892 for his part in the Liberator Building Society fraud. Hobbs was released on licence after serving six years of his sentence.

Aerial view of Norbury in 1928. The London Road runs north to south. The large meadow is the sports ground, once part of the grounds of Norbury Hall, which is visible through the trees behind. Norbury Hall was built in 1802 by William Coles and the grounds improved by the next occupant, Richard Sanderson, who laid out the gardens and created a lake. The grounds are now a public park and Norbury Hall is a private nursing home.

Passengers boarding the tram for a summer's day out which, apart from the bicycle, is the only vehicle in the London Road – a complete contrast to traffic conditions on the A23 in the year 2000. The London Road became a turnpike in 1718 when the Surrey & Sussex Turnpike Trust was established. The milestone on the left-hand kerb dates from the turnpike days. It indicates 7 miles to Whitehall and $7\frac{1}{2}$ miles to the Royal Exchange. The Norbury Hall sports ground was once known as Milestone Meadow.

Norbury Library was built on the corner of Beatrice Avenue and opened with appropriate ceremony on Saturday 31 May 1931 by the Mayor, Alderman T. Arthur Lewis. The houses in this photograph have recently been replaced by flats.

Originally known as 'the little church up the hill', St Philip's church, in Beech Avenue, was originally a chapel of ease for Christ Church at Broad Green, only gaining its own separate parish in 1912. The land on which it stood was donated by Alderman G.J. Allen, a Norbury resident and Mayor of Croydon in 1898-99. The first section of the church was completed in 1902 and the westernmost bays of the nave were completed in 1935. The join is noticeable in the slight colour difference of the roof tiles. The houses which now stand to the right of the church were not yet built. St Philip's is known for its choir, called Libera.

The Wesleyan Methodist church was built on the corner of Pollards Hill North with London Road in 1905. Owing to the costs of maintenance of this unusual building, it was demolished in 1977. Worship continues in the church hall next door. The site is now occupied by a health centre.

The roads of the Pollards Hill estate were originally laid out in 1867 by the Metropolitan Land & Finance Company. Subsequent development did not commence until thirty years later, and then only in a piecemeal fashion. Pollards Hill East, seen in this photograph, was finally completed in 1914. The summit of Pollards Hill was saved from development through the generosity of Sir Fredrick Edridge, who donated the land to Croydon Corporation as a recreation ground, formally opened on 2 July 1913.

Frank Chown was one of the land developers in Norbury. In his sales brochure Chown extolled the delights of Norbury, and in particular Pollards Hill, in very rhapsodic language; he described the area as 'a peaceful haven of leisure and rest'.

On a wet day in March 1931 a shelter was opened in the recreation ground on the summit of Pollards Hill. This was given by local residents in memory of Dr McWilliams, a much respected local doctor.

By the late twenties shopping parades had been developed between Warwick Road and Melrose Avenue. Sainsbury's owned a shop here on the left and the author remembers the marble slab counters and the bacon slicers.

The land belonging to Norbury Hall once extended almost to Warwick Road. It was known as the Norbury Park Estate. Following James Hobbs' imprisonment for fraud, this estate was divided into plots and sold at auction for development, with the result that houses of varied designs were built. The backs of the houses in Ederline Avenue were built with balconies to overlook the tennis club and cricket ground.

Norbury was noted for its golf courses. The North Surrey Golf Club with its entrance in Green Lane was created on land originally endowed to Pembroke College, Cambridge. During the Second World War the golf course was requisitioned for allotments and after the war it became a public open space now known as Norbury Park.

Green Lane was just that – an ancient lane that ran from the turnpike road at Lower Streatham to Colliers Water Lane and the lower slopes of the Norwood Hills. According to a survey in 1867 the width varied from 5ft to 29ft. It was used as an alternative route to Croydon when the River Graveney was in flood.

So, Green Lane, which was once a quiet country track, by the 1930s had become an important thoroughfare. Much of the housing leading off Green Lane around Gibson's Hill and Briar Avenue was built by Wates. Nearby Covington Way was named after Stenton Covington who, through strenuous efforts, saved Norwood Grove for public use. The General bus is on route 159, which started as a Saturday service in 1929 and then ran daily from 1934.

Two
Galpins Road to the Pond

Galpins Road led across the fields from London Road down to Mitcham Common. It possibly took its name from Gilpins Farm situated on the edge of the Common. The photograph was taken around 1905 from the corner with London Road. Development would commence very shortly.

Alongside housing development parades of shops were built along the main thoroughfares. The corner shops between Headcorn Road and Galpins Road were built in 1912 but a delay took place in the construction of the central units, which were not completed until 1925. The dairy on the corner, owned by the Improved New Milk Delivery Co., advertised the fact that they sold their milk in sealed bottles rather than ladled into the consumer's own containers. The business was later taken over first by Welford's then the Home Counties Dairy.

Leander Road in course of completion in 1908. The trees in the distance were felled when the houses of Silverleigh Road and Mayfield Road were constructed about ten years later.

Grosvenor House on the corner of Warwick Road was built for Paul Augustus Peacock, a partner in the firm of Nurdin & Peacock, in 1876. Paul Peacock died in tragic circumstances in the house in 1900. In 1914 the nuns of the Ursuline Order established a school there. From 1940 the building was home to St Christopher's, a special needs school. The flats of St Christopher's Gardens now occupy the site.

The nuns extended the premises and the opening ceremony took place on 9 July 1927 in which the Roman Catholic Bishop of Southwark, Dr Amigo, and the Mayor of Croydon, Alderman A.J. Camden Field, took part.

The area bordering Winterbourne Road, Wiltshire Road, and Bridport Road was known as the 'Greenbroom' after the shrub that grew there in profusion. Small terraced hoses were constructed from the 1880s. This view looks west along Winterbourne Road at the crossroads with Wiltshire Road and dates from around 1900, certainly prior to the development of 1908. On the left is the corrugated iron building of the Mission established by St Saviour's parish in 1889, out of which grew the new parish of St Stephen's (see chapter 12).

Local children have gathered in Winterbourne Road for the cameraman but the occasion is not known. It illustrates clearly children's fashions of the Edwardian era.

28

Winterbourne Schools opened in 1907. The infants' school was housed in its own separate building while the girls' and boys' schools were based in the main block. Heath Clark School occupied the 'annexe' building on the same site. Even today Winterbourne Schools, apart from the infants, are the only single-sex primary schools in the country. At Easter 1936 twenty-three girls visited Paris for a week. They set off by coach from outside the school on 8 April. Alderman Mrs Bessie Roberts took a keen interest in the Girls' School and she came to see the party off.

Class 12 of Winterbourne Boys' School in 1962 with the author sitting third from the left in the front row. Reginald King was the form teacher at the time and had held the post as deputy head of the school since 1951.

Thornton Heath School had many homes since its founding in 1884 by Mr A.C. Dent. In 1888 the school was in Quadrant Road but by 1915 it was based in The Grove, seen here. The house probably dated to the 1800s but it was also marked on the map compiled for the Croydon Enclosure Award of 1797, when it was known as Pound House, due to its proximity to the pound on the heath. One of the owners was Thomas Turner, a noted veterinary surgeon of the nineteenth century who became the first president of the Royal College of Veterinary Surgeons. The Principal of Thornton Heath School was Mr J.D. Davies whose son, Peter. provided this photograph. In 1928 the school relocated to a nearby property 'Silverleigh' near Goldwell Road and finally transferred to Brigstock Road in 1935 until its closure in 1939. After The Grove was demolished in 1928, S & R G Everett & Co., makers of hypodermic instruments, built a new factory on the site, the lodge to The Grove being incorporated within the factory complex. Today the fast food outlet of McDonalds is on the factory site.

London Road in the snow, on the morning of 1 April 1917. Billboards have been erected, behind which the terraced houses between Oaklands Avenue and Langdale Road were later to be built. As a blackout precaution, the headlamp of the tram is covered by a stencil with the letter 'P', indicating it is bound for Purley.

The Exchange parade of shops between Malvern Road and Langdale Road was built in 1906 following the break-up of the Thornton House estate. On the corner with Malvern Road was Welfords Dairy. The postcard was sent to Miss Tudball in Bristol, whose family occupied No. 3 The Exchange.

Albert E. Tudball ran a tailoring business in shop premises at No. 3 The Exchange. Serge was a twilled worsted fabric.

Langdale Road, *c*. 1910. Thornton House, once owned by Henry Crowley of the brewery company of Crowley Brothers, is shown on the Croydon Commons Enclosure Award map of 1800. After Henry's widow, Elizabeth, died in 1900 the house was demolished and Malvern, Lyndhurst, Langdale, Beverstone, Weybridge, Woodland and Maplethorpe Roads were laid out. Part of the estate around Nutfield Road was sold for gravel extraction prior to house building. The late George Goring, who lived in Winterbourne Road around 1900, recalled that the ponds created as a result of gravel extraction became a source of delight for local children and a cause for their late arrival at Ecclesbourne School.

The Thornton Heath Evangelical Free Church began as a mission of the Congregational church at Campbell Road and met at the Oxford Coffee Rooms by the Pond. The church was established on the corner of Malvern Road in this building in October 1904. The present church building replaced the mission hall in 1954.

Dovercourt, a mid-nineteenth-century mansion, stood opposite what is now the Gala Bingo Hall. It was the home of Thomas Farley, who occupied it from about 1850 until his death in July 1881. His widow, Frances, and daughter continued to live there. It was demolished in 1926 and Dovercourt Avenue was built on the site. The gibbet once stood on this site.

With the growth of the film industry during the 1920s and 30s most communities had a cinema. Owned by A.C. Mathews, who also operated cinemas at Upper Norwood and Sydenham, the State cinema opened on Boxing Day 1932. However, it was bought by the Granada group and renamed the Granada from 1949. Like many Granada cinemas in the 1970s, it was turned into a bingo hall. The building has recently been demolished and an apartment block built on the site.

Three
Thornton Heath Pond

Thornton Heath Pond was a well-known landmark and it is thought that originally it was used as a source of water by the colliers of the Great North Wood. The pond would certainly have been used to water cattle and other animals grazing on the heath. The area today is still known as 'The Pond' to distinguish it from 'The High Street' over a mile away at the opposite end of Brigstock Road. The photograph dates from the 1880s.

An aerial view taken around 1925, featuring the Pond in the centre. The London Road runs from the top right to the bottom. Trafford Road/Mayfield Road, on the extreme left, is partly laid out. Leander and Headcorn Roads are at the top. A fair has been set up at the side of Fairlands Avenue, which is under construction. In the centre The Grove estate is being developed by the firm of Bates and Duckit, while to the right Dovercourt is about to disappear with the construction of Dovercourt Avenue. Limes Parade is also under construction on the corner of Brigstock Road.

The Pond provided the perfect background for many picturesque photographs, including this scene with groups of children.

The ornamental fountain that graced the pond was erected to commemorate the Golden Jubilee of Queen Victoria in 1887. It cost about £80 and was paid for by local residents and landowners, while Croydon Council authorized the cleaning out of the pond at a cost of £50! On Thursday 27 October 1887 invited guests, including the Mayor, local councillors and subscribers, partook of lunch at the Wheatsheaf after which the fountain was turned on with due ceremony. A telegram was sent to the Queen at Balmoral informing her of the event in her honour.

3826. THE POND, THORNTON HEATH. CROFT'S COPYRIGHT.

The Wheatsheaf, built in the early nineteenth century, was a coaching inn on the turnpike road. Behind the Wheatsheaf in Willett Road was the blacksmith's shop.

Many of the small cottages around the pond dated from the early years of the nineteenth century. Bailey's boot and shoe repair business occupied the cottage in the middle of this picture. Apart from the adjacent house to the right, later to be obscured by the facade of an estate agents, none survive today.

THE POND, THORNTON HEATH.

The two shops on the left still survive and carry the date 1887. The Oxford Coffee Rooms occupied one of these for many years. The Plough and Harrow, a Crowleys public house, was rebuilt in the 1930s. Raymead Avenue now cuts through on the extreme right.

The shops in this view are still there today, with only the tram and the pond to date this view to the late 1930s. In 1953, to cope with increasing post-war traffic volumes, the pond was filled in, the roads widened, and a one-way system created around the pond. An ornamental garden was created.

A group of regulars setting off, possibly for a football match judging by the rosettes, from outside the Plough and Harrow public house. During recent years the pub became the Indian Queen and is now the Dosti Nouvelle Fusion restaurant.

With the introduction of the Austin 7 and Morris 8 in the 1920s, motoring was beginning to be within reach of those who were not rich and famous. Jack Feathers has on display an MG, one of the first Morris Minors, as well as a Standard, Wolseley and Riley. A car dealer still occupies the site today.

Four
London Road

51860 Thornton Heath Tramway Depot

Alexandra Buildings were built in 1901 and named after the new Queen, wife of King Edward VII. In the centre is Brigstock Villa, the headquarters of the Croydon Corporation Tramways. The depot was behind. The depot complex was replaced by the bus garage in 1951.

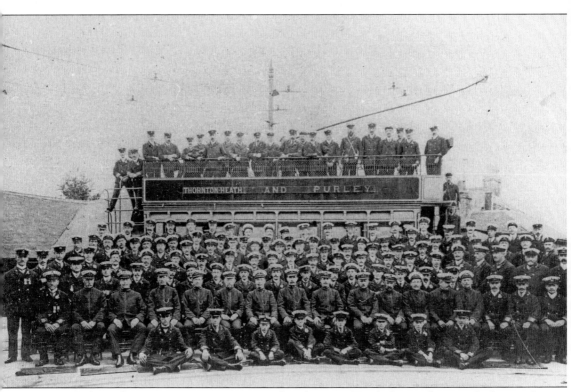

Staff of Croydon Corporation Tramways at the Thornton Heath depot, photographed soon after the system commenced operation in 1901. The first trams arrived at Thornton Heath Pond in 1879. They were small single-decker cars of primitive design. By 1883, two-horse double-decker cars began operating up Brigstock Road to the High Street. In 1900 Croydon Corporation acquired and electrified the system. On 26 September 1901, new electric tramcars ran through from Purley to Norbury, with Brigstock Road electrified in 1902. All the tram and bus undertakings around London were amalgamated into the London Passenger Transport Board in 1933. Because of the great crowds who travelled on the first Sunday of operation, a queuing system was adopted.

Lifeboat Day took place on Wednesday 22 July 1908. There were two processions: one in the south of the borough and the other in the north. The processions included fire engines, mounted police, various floats, decorated motorcars and bicycles as well as a decorated tramcar which was illuminated at night by dozens of coloured lights. The northern procession featured the Southend lifeboat drawn by eight horses with crew in seagoing clothing. Here the procession is turning out from Brigstock Road into London Road. The house on the left was called The Limes. Crowds turned out to watch the parades and a holiday was declared for the afternoon so that schoolchildren could join in the fun.

This view is from almost the same position as the picture above, but is around twenty years younger. Limes Parade now stands in the front garden of The Limes. The gates of Brigstock House, one-time home of Joshua Allder, still survive on the right but only two years later, in 1930, the shops on the corner of Brigstock Road would be built.

The last trams in Thornton Heath ran on 7 April 1951. Here the last tram is turning out from Brigstock Road into the London Road. The crowds saying farewell would have had no idea that trams would one day return to the streets of Croydon, nearly fifty years later.

Large detached or semi-detached villas, many complete with coach house and stable, lined each side of the London Road south from the Pond. During the early nineteenth century this section of London Road became known as Millionaire's Row due to the wealth of many of the residents. Until 1890 the postal address was just 'Thornton Heath'.

Maypole dancing at the League of Nations Fête held on 26 June 1926 at Dunheved House, the residence of Alderman Southwell.

The Devonshire Arms and the parade of shops, seen here in February 1961, were demolished as part of the Mayday Hospital (now Croydon University Hospital) redevelopment in the 1980s. One of the statues of the doctors' surgery fell down and the other removed in 1970. Edgar Browne, the son of Hablot K. Browne better known as 'Phiz', the illustrator of Charles Dickens' books, lived nearby

Aerial view of Mayday Hospital taken in 1920. The hospital was opened on 16 May 1885, but at the time of the photograph, Mayday was still known as the Croydon Union Infirmary, the Poor Law hospital administered by the Board of Guardians. In 1923 it was renamed Mayday Hospital and is now a major teaching hospital. Bensham Lane snakes across the photograph; at one time it was an ancient lane leading across the medieval Common Fields. In the nineteenth century much of the area around Bensham Lane was given over to market gardens. Members of the Randall and Fowles families continued to cultivate market gardens right up until 1937. Woodcroft Road, which runs to the east of the hospital, was previously known as Edridge Road, its name being changed in 1939 to avoid confusion with Edridge Road in Croydon.

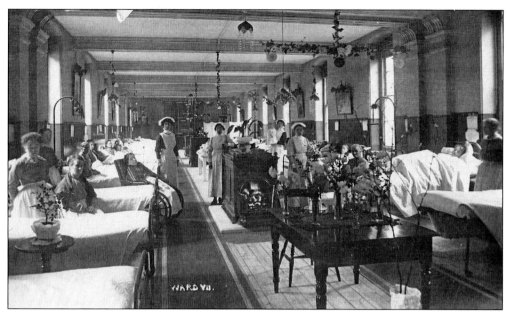

Ward VII of the Croydon Union Infirmary, the Poor Law Hospital.

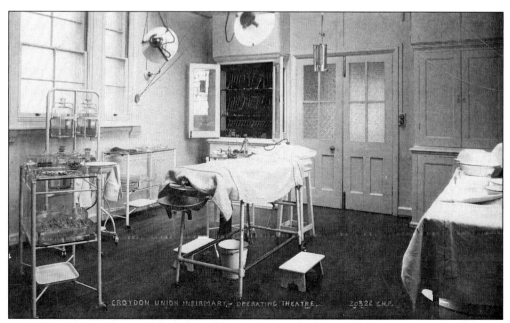

The operating theatre of the Croydon Union Infirmary in 1921. At that time operations were only carried out once every three weeks. The maids, employed by the Union, had to get up at 4.30 a.m. to scrub the floor and light the fire to ensure the theatre was clean and warm.

Alderman Bessie Roberts at the opening of the Nurses' Home in 1930.

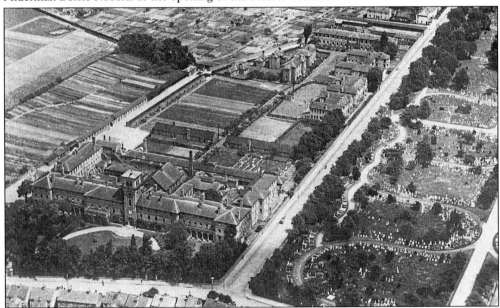

At the bottom left of this view was the workhouse of the Croydon Union, built in 1865 to replace the old building situated at Duppas Hill. It was intended to house the able-bodied poor who had no means of support. It was supported by the rates of the districts which comprised the Croydon Union. These were Croydon, Penge, Addington, Sanderstead, Coulsdon, Mitcham, Merton, Morden, Beddington, Wallington and Woodmansterne. In 1923 the workhouse was renamed Queens Hospital, catering mainly for the elderly and infirm. A certain stigma from the workhouse association remained for many years. To the right is Queens Road cemetery, opened for burials in 1861. With the workhouse and cemetery next to each other, Queens Road was known locally as 'Death and Poverty Row'.

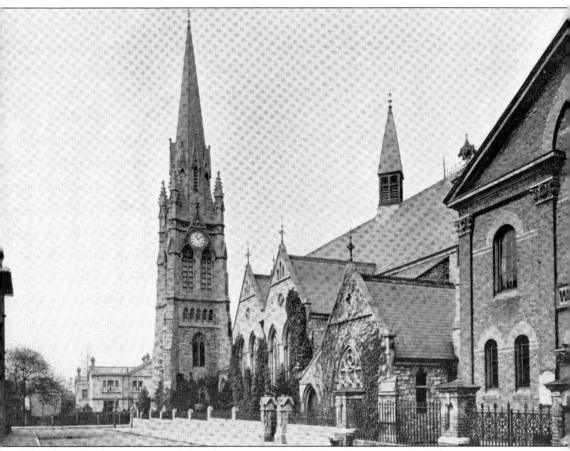

West Croydon Congregational church was opened in 1886 and constructed of Kentish ragstone and Bath stone. The church members originally met in the hall behind the church in Campbell Road. A carillon was presented to the church for which the tower had to be strengthened to carry the weight of the bells. One prominent member of this church was Croydon's first mayor, Jabez Spencer Balfour, indicted in the Liberator Building Society scandal in 1892. Since 1982 the church has been the Oshwal Mahajanwadi, a Jain Temple. In the London Road stands The Cedars. Midhurst Avenue now cuts through the grounds of The Cedars.

Now known as Holy Saviour following the closure of Holy Trinity, Selhurst, St Saviour's church was consecrated in 1867 but the tall tower and spire were not added until fifteen years later. It was built on land bequeathed by Newman Smith who lived at nearby Croydon Lodge.

Summer camp was a highlight on the Girl Guides' calendar. The girls, together with their leaders, of the 41st Croydon troop based at St Saviour's church are preparing to leave Seabrook camp in 1938.

The children of St Saviour's School in 1928. The school closed shortly after the opening of Elmwood Primary Council School in Lodge Road.

Anne and Ellen Sturton, spinster sisters, founded the North Park Ladies' College in one of the large houses in Elmwood Road in 1889. The school later transferred to 240 London Road on the corner of Campbell Road. Some of the pupils were boarders. In 1910 the school occupied the detached house 1A Malvern Road, but with new principals, Miss Monday and Miss Poole. Marion Monday had previously been a pupil at the school. It closed in 1939.

Robert Kynaston and his family lived at 2 Bensham Villas, 236 London Road. He died in 1874 but the family continued to live there until 1923. One of the daughters, Beatrice, was an accomplished photographer and a number of her photographs appear in this book. Their house, along with the remainder of these fine villas between Campbell Road and Broad Green Avenue were demolished in the late 1970s to make way for City House, the UK headquarters of Philips Electronics.

Five

Broad Green

Broad Green, c. 1905. Sumner Road, leading off to Mitcham Road on the left, was named after Archbishop John Bird Sumner.

Broad Green Lodge stood on the west side of London Road. Here is the garden front of the house facing westwards about 1870 from a group of photographs believed to have been taken by Joshua Allder. The Sargood family were living here at the time.

The grounds of Broad Green Lodge included a lake and rose gardens. There was a large field behind the house where the children of Reedham Orphanage came for their summer outing.

Broad Green Lodge was up for sale in 1900 and Greenside Road was laid out shortly afterwards. The clothing that the boys are wearing was typical of middle-class children. See also Melfort Road on p. 84.

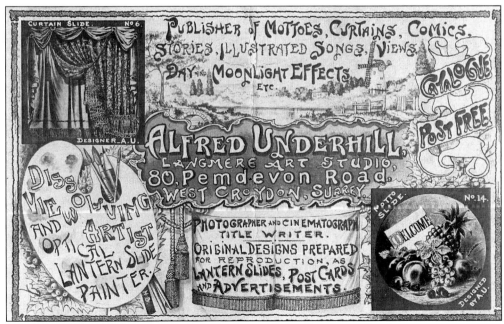

A business postcard for Alfred Underhill, who resided in Pemdevon Road.

London Road at the corner of Broad Green Avenue, c. 1910. Facilities for the motorist were gradually increasing as evidenced by the advertisement for motor spirit. In this view, though, the car still has to compete with horse-drawn traffic.

The Dennett Hall was erected in 1888 by the Croydon Domestic Mission of the Free Christian Church (a Unitarian church) with its objects being 'the intellectual, moral and religious improvement of the neighbourhood, and the amelioration of its condition, irrespective of creed.' This Mission ran a coal club, clothing club and sewing club as well as a free library. Demolished in 1986, Nos 17-19 now occupy the site. Only fresh produce is on display for the Harvest Thanksgiving with not a packet or tin can to be seen!

The earliest record of the Half Moon Public House dates from 1515 although the present building dates from the nineteenth century. Batchelars also owned a store in North End, Croydon later acquired by Kennards and now Debenhams.

The Star Hotel at Broad Green has its origins in a beer shop run by William Hetherington in 1835. The present building dates from 1892. The 'star' was taken down as unsafe. It is now the Broad Green Tavern.

Part of the ABC (Associated British Cinemas) circuit, the Savoy cinema opened its doors on 9 March 1936 with seating for 2,276 patrons and became one of the top three Croydon cinemas along with the Odeon and Davis Theatre. A severe fire occurred at the end of March 1953 but the theatre was rebuilt and several live shows took place in the 1960s, featuring among others Cliff Richard and the Beatles. The Savoy later became part of the Cannon Group in 1986 then the Safari but was demolished in 2008 and Gary Court built on the site.

A 1950s view of Broad Green. Unfortunately the section of Royal Parade on the right was burnt down in the riots of 8/9 July 2012.

After the demolition of Broad Green Place, Kidderminster and Nova Roads were built in 1902. A brilliantly exuberant Royal Parade was erected along the London Road frontage of the estate.

An illustration of the garden front of Broad Green House taken from the sales particulars of December 1891. The house was built for Alexander Caldcleugh in 1807 after purchasing the Rectory manor estate which extended at one time to North End, Croydon. Following the 1891 sale Chatfield and Montague Roads were laid out. In 1929 Dr J. Gregg established one of his secretarial and commercial schools in Broad Green House. Gregg devised a shorthand system as a rival to Pitman's. After the war Broad Green College moved into the building but relocated in 1964 to Normanton Road when redevelopment took place. Zodiac House occupies the site now.

The entrance lodge in the London Road, *c.* 1890. The horse tram track is in the foreground.

The corner of St James's Road and London Road. The driver of R. White's cart is making his way back to the company's Morland Road premises. Most of the buildings still exist although the majority have had new shop fronts added. Until the mid-nineteenth century Broad Green consisted of a small settlement on the edge of Croydon Common, the town centre only commencing when one reached North End.

Originally known as Brooke House after John Brooke, a cooper from Southwark, the house name was changed to Broad Green Place in 1851. The main drive led from St James's Road at the Windmill Road junction. On the death of the last owner, Elizabeth Cox (grand-daughter of John Brooke), the houses in Nova and Hathaway Roads were built. The Cox family cared passionately for mistreated horses. The horses which they adopted were allowed to graze in the field in front of the garden fence.

The junction of St James's Road and Windmill Road in the 1890s. Lodge Road leads off to the left into the exclusive housing estate of North Park, built after 1867, while the close-boarded gates lead into the grounds of Croydon Lodge.

A view taken nearly fifteen years later from the same point as the photograph above. The houses in Windmill Road have only just been built. St Michael's and All Angels Church School was erected in the angle of the roads and opened in 1908. The school closed in 1976 because of insufficient numbers on the school roll and because of the cramped nature of the site.

St Mary's Maternity Hospital was established in Argyll House in St James's Road. In 1928 it was considerably enlarged with a bequest from Cllr Charles Heath Clark. It closed in 1985 with the transfer to the new maternity unit at Mayday Hospital.

The eastern half of Elmwood Road, built on the site of Croydon Lodge in the 1920s.

Christ Church, built by the Simeon Trustees in 1852 in Sumner Road. The most notable in-cumbent of the church was the Revd Octavius Bathurst Byers, who established many missions in the developing areas around Boston Road and Thornton Heath Pond. He was also Croydon's longest serving minister. Christ Church suffered a disastrous fire in 1986 and the remains were demolished to make way for a new purpose-built church and hall.

The Canterbury Arms on the corner of Sumner and Lambeth Roads, c. 1913. The pub has been renamed the Nowhere Inn Particular.

Six

West Thornton

Numbers 29 and 31 Thornton Road were the oldest houses standing in Thornton Heath in recent years. Number 31 probably dated back to the early eighteenth century. They were demolished when the bus garage was extended in 1978.

Waddon Marsh Lane led westward from the Pond to Waddon. The lane was renamed Thornton Road as development encroached, but even in this photograph, taken after 1900, the road is still very rural. Gonville Road leads off to the right.

Thornton Road, looking eastwards towards the Pond from roughly the same spot as the photograph above. The large house on the left is still there.

Thornton Road was widened in the early twenties as part of the by-pass scheme for Croydon and for traffic to Croydon Aerodrome, the customs airport for London. St Jude's church is in course of construction. The congregation of St Jude's first worshipped in the large hall, built in 1911, shown here on the corner of Limpsfield Road.

A single-row seed drill in use on rather infertile-looking land off Thornton Road, c. 1911. In the background can be seen houses in Aurelia Road, the chapel of Mitcham Road cemetery and John Jakson's peppermint distillery. This land became the crematorium and cemetery extension opened in 1933.

The origins of St Jude's church lay in an iron Mission Room of Christ Church in Stanley Grove in 1886. A temporary church in Thornton Road was erected in 1911 that subsequently became the church hall. Finally a new church building was begun in 1927. This photograph shows G.H. Redwood, Deputy Provincial Grand Master of the Freemasons for Surrey, laying the foundation stone on 11 June 1927.

In September 1928, soon after its completion, St Jude's suffered a very serious fire destroying the newly completed roof. It was soon rebuilt but the church's consecration was consequently delayed until the following year.

The junction of Mitcham Road and Thornton Road in 1955 shortly after the roundabout was completed. Lombard Banking occupied the office block at this roundabout, giving it the local name of Lombard roundabout, one of the busiest in the Croydon area. Behind are the cooling towers of Croydon B power station, demolished in 1991. The trolleybus wires were for route 630 from West Croydon to near Willesden Junction.

Old farm cottages, part of Waddon Marsh Farm, at the junction of Mitcham Road and Waddon Marsh Lane, c. 1895. The Lombard office block was built on this site.

The junction of Canterbury Road and Wortley Road in 1910. Canterbury Road, Boston Road and Stanley Road were developed from the 1850s onwards, having been laid out in the former grounds of Weller House. The firm of F. Musgrove, baker, had taken over from Robert Mead in 1901. The Musgrove family continued the business until 1921 when Thomas Brooks took over.

John Jakson's peppermint distillery in Mitcham Road. Mitcham became famous in the nineteenth century for the production of lavender and peppermint oils. The fragrance from the lavender and peppermint fields would waft across to Thornton Heath, as recorded by H.C. Barnard when staying with his grandfather in the 1890s. By that time the largest producer was John Jakson's distillery which stood on the site where Challenge House is today. The company closed down after the Second World War, by which time most of the land around the distillery had been built on.

The Accounting and Tabulating Works in Aurelia Road. The 'Acc & Tab', as the company was known, employed many people living in Thornton Heath. In 1959 the factory was taken over by the International Computers and Tabulation Company.

Wildbore's Lane in 1884. This was the old name for the footpath that runs behind Harcourt Road. It continued across Canterbury Road to Mitcham Road along the line of Sutherland Road. The lane was named after Dr Richard Wildbore, the physician who attended Edward Weller of nearby Weller House.

The 1920s saw the building of most of the factory estates on the western side of Thornton Road, including the premises of John Bennett (Croydon) Ltd, a haulage contractor, seen here in 1926.

Seven

Colliers Water Lane and Brigstock Road

The Brigstock Arms, a Noakes house, showing the polychrome decorative brickwork used before the application of stucco cladding. The pub was built on the corner of the newly constructed section of Brigstock Road and Colliers Water Lane in 1869. The name Brigstock comes from a seventeenth-century brewing family. The building is now part of a Pentecostal church.

Colliers Water Lane was another old highway which ran through fields and farmland leading from the Pond eastward towards the Norwood Hills. It then extended along what was to become Brigstock Road and Thornton Heath High Street. The name bears witness to the charcoal burners, or 'colliers' as they were known, who plied their trade in the Great North Wood. Water to damp down their fires was probably collected from the Norbury Brook rather than the ancient pond on the heath. The white-painted building in the middle distance is Lilac Cottage.

Lilac Cottage in Colliers Water Lane (seen here c. 1913) was part of the Thornton House estate.

The terraced houses on the right were constructed in 1906, shortly after the sale of the Thornton House estate had taken place. The open space on the left remained until the 1960s.

A typical wooden-clad labourer's cottage that bordered Colliers Water Lane. Two groups of mid-nineteenth-century cottages still survive today.

The narrowness of Brigstock Road only allowed for tramway passing loops. Behind the wall on the left was The Limes, once owned by J. West, who was responsible for much of the nineteenth-century development in the road.

The completed fire station with its new Dennis motor fire engine outside.

ONE LAYING. .AFTER the CEREMONY. NEW FIRE STATION OCT 1913

The laying of the foundation stone of the new fire station on 13 October 1913. This station, complete with a new Dennis motor fire engine, replaced the one in Beulah Road run by the Volunteer Fire Brigade. The opening took place on 8 July 1914. Braidwood House nows stands on the site.

After much public pressure a new library, replacing the temporary one established in the Polytechnic building in the High Street, was finally built on land adjoining the site for the new fire station. The total cost was £5,000, with funding of £4,200 provided by the Andrew Carnegie Trust. It was opened on 8 July 1914.

Wyncott College, run by Frank and Ann Banks, occupied the large villa on the corner of Quadrant Road. It was one of many small private schools that existed before the Second World War. The author's father attended this school. The building was destroyed by the V1 incident depicted on p. 117.

Gilbert Matthers originally opened his music school in Bensham Manor Road. A branch of his music school opened in North End, Croydon. He later transferred to these premises in Brigstock Road. Bernard Matthers took over running the School of Music after his father's death just before the war.

Matthers' students performing at Croydon's Public Hall in December 1913.

Brook Road, named after the Norbury Brook that flows behind the houses on the west side of the road, was first laid out as Beulah Road East, being an extension of Beulah Road over the railway line and across Melfort Road. Carew Road was named after the Carew family who were the Lords of the Manor of Norbury. The 1868 Ordnance Survey map indicates that there was a brickfield on this site.

The entrance to Thornton Heath Recreation Ground at the end of Carew Road.

Bowling Green in Recreation Ground, Thornton Heath.

The Bowling Green in the recreation ground was laid out in 1908 and formally opened by the Mayor of Croydon on 3 June 1908.

Newton & Gutteridge   Recreation Ground, Thornton Heath   4350

Thornton Heath Recreation Ground was one of the earlier open spaces to be acquired by Croydon Council. The first section off Carew Road was opened in 1884 but after complaints about insufficient room to play cricket, a further section was opened in February 1892. A right of way forms the division between the two areas of land. The trees planted to line the path have now grown into maturity. The bandstand was situated on the site of today's children's playground.

Melfort Road ran parallel with the railway line from Brigstock Road to Norbury. The children are wearing smart clothes even while out playing. Iron hoops were the item to have.

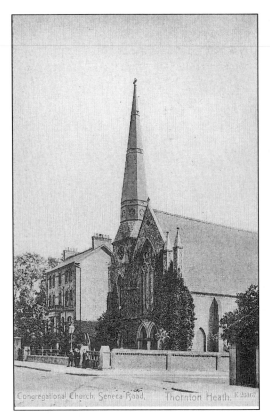

St John's Congregational church began as St John's free church in 1868, with Anglican and Non-conformist services until St Paul's was built in 1872. In 1949 a number of churches in Croydon were subject to arson attacks, including St John's, in March of that year. The church remains today as a member of the Congregational Union rather than joining the United Reformed Church when Congregationalists and English Presbyterians merged in 1972.

The Parade, Brigstock Road, dates from 1899. New parades of shops sprang up along the main thoroughfares, each with their butchers, bakers, greengrocers, confectioners, newsagents etc. With no 'mod cons', the Edwardian housewife did not have time to go far, and perishables had to be bought daily.

Thornton Heath station was opened on 1 December 1862 with the opening of the Selhurst to Streatham Common branch of the London, Brighton and South Coast Railway. The original station building, as seen here, was situated on the up side of the tracks. The frozen food store Iceland now occupies the original station yard.

Following the quadrupling of the line between Selhurst and Balham in 1903, Thornton Heath station was rebuilt with the ticket and parcels offices situated on the bridge. This early postcard view from around 1904 shows the station building. The horse-bus is about to set off for South Norwood.

Commuters waiting at Thornton Heath station about 1916. With so many men serving in the forces there were many more opportunities for women to work in London offices. The overhead catenary was part of the London, Brighton and South Coast Railway's electrification scheme.

The railways provided much employment and even a small station had staff to deal not only with passengers, but also parcels and freight. The staff of Thornton Heath station pose for this photograph taken in around 1910. In the middle sits Edward Shepherd, the stationmaster.

The Old Farm House, Thornton Heath.
(Residence of John Gilpin.)

The ancient building of Colliers Water Farm, built around 1590, stood where Tesco supermarket is now. Many legends concerned the farmhouse, some involving the charcoal burners, or colliers, of the nearby Great North Wood. Later still the old farm was believed to be the haunt of smugglers and footpads, as the house had a secret staircase to the roof, thereby providing a place of refuge. At the junction of two winding lanes this was a remote part of Croydon. Note the flint and brick wall; this type of construction using local materials was common in the Croydon area.

The demise of Colliers Water Farm, with its 'for sale' boards outside. The young lad and the pony and trap are standing at the junction with Parchmore Road. To the left the horse-tram track leads down Brigstock Road towards the station.

An aerial view of Thornton Heath station with its two goods yards. The High Street leads to the bottom left from the Clock Tower, standing at the end of the green. Woodville Road is seen leading to the bottom right.

Horse trams began operation to Thornton Heath High Street in 1881. Here a two-horse 'garden seat' tram is proceeding to Croydon. On the left of the picture is the first section of the Poly-technic building, opened in 1893, while the trees on the right are part of the grounds of Cotford House.

The Prince of Wales pub, dating from the 1860s, was a Nalder and Collyers house. For the last seventy years, it has been home to the Croydon Amateur Boxing Club and prior to closure had its boxing ring in the gym on the first floor. The Clock Tower was erected in 1900 and cost £300. Half the cost was met by the Corporation, with the remainder by public subscription. The B-type bus is about to commence its long journey to Shepherds Bush on the Sunday extension from Streatham on route 49 that lasted from 1913 to 1922.

Cotford Parade was built in the grounds of Cotford House in 1933. The line of lock-up shops on the left, erected after Colliers Water Farm was demolished, included many coal merchants' order offices. The coal was delivered by goods train to the railway goods yard behind. The whole site is now occupied by Tesco.

Eight

Thornton Heath High Street

William and George Lack's shop occupied a considerable frontage from 115-121 High Street. The store is lit up for their sale in 1935.

A vendor of whirligig toys selling his wares opposite the Polytechnic building on 7 August 1912.

A procession organized by the International Peace Movement wends its way into the High Street in 1930.

The swimming baths in the High Street were opened in 1897 and besides the main pool included private baths for men and women. During the winter months the baths hall was used as a ballroom.

The baths have hosted a number of events, including galas and dances for which the bath has been boarded over. On 29 July 1956 a mass baptism of Jehovah's Witnesses took place; this view shows the queue outside. The site is now occupied by the Thornton Heath Leisure Centre incorporating a new swimming pool.

Thornton Heath High Street developed as the commercial centre of the district following the opening of the railway line and the subsequent increase in population. Hughes' Drapery Stores on the corner of Grange Park Road, on the extreme right, was demolished to make way for the new Central Cinema which opened in 1911.

After rebuilding in 1921 the Central Cinema became the Pavilion and even had its own tiny orchestra to accompany silent films. After closure in 1956 it reopened as the Pullman in 1958 with final closure in 1960. The front section is now a take-away restaurant.

Even in 1913 Lilly & Skinner and Freeman, Hardy & Willis were household names. Carcasses of meat were hung up outside the butchers; although unhygienic by today's standards, this was normal practice then.

The Electric Palace on the corner of The Retreat was Thornton Heath's first picture house and owned at first by Electric Palaces Ltd. The auditorium was behind the entrance hall. The slogan over the decorative plasterwork at first floor level read 'The World and its Wonders Week by Week'. In 1927 it became a dance hall, the Palais de Danse, with, it is believed, the first sprung dance floor in the country.

Whitehorse Manor house and farm stood at the corner of Colliers Water Lane and Whitehorse Lane. The manor took its name from Walter Whitehorse, shield-bearer to Edward III, into whose possession the manor came in 1368. The manor house had the date 1604 cut on its front. The house and farm buildings were demolished at the end of the nineteenth century.

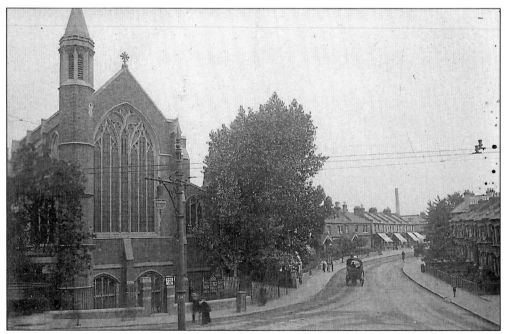

Technically just within the postal district of South Norwood, St Alban's church dominates the scene at the junction of High Street, Grange Road, Whitehorse Road and Whitehorse Lane which here leads off to the right. Sir Ninian Comper, the celebrated architect, designed the church, which was completed in 1894.

The horse trams terminated at the junction of High Street and Whitehorse Lane. This is one of Beatrice Kynaston's photographs taken in the 1890s.

The tram terminus outside St Alban's church, with one of the larger Croydon Corporation trams about to return to Croydon via the Pond and London Road.

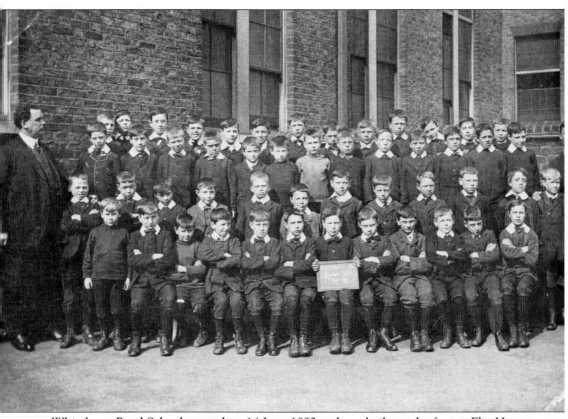

Whitehorse Road School opened on 14 June 1892 and was built on the former Elm House estate. As with many schools at the time, boys and girls were educated separately. Here the boys of Standard IV are assembled for the class photograph in 1911. In 1955 the school, now known as Whitehorse Manor, bcame solely a primary school. The senior boys transferred to Tavistock School.

Promising children as young as fourteen were trained as pupil teachers, spending half their time at training schools and the remainder teaching in schools. In 1900 there were 107 trainees at the Whitehorse Road Pupil Teacher Centre.

Girls studying domestic science at Lady Edridge School, Clifton Road, shortly after it obtained grammar school status in 1951. The school first opened in 1920 in Selhurst Road and was named after the wife of Alderman Sir Frederick Edridge. It closed in 1986.

The tram route which extended from the High Street terminus along Whitehorse Road to the junction with the Crystal Palace/Penge routes at The Gloster had a very chequered career. It opened in 1906. However, due to lack of custom it closed in 1908 but reopened for a short time in 1911, finally closing in 1913. The area at the junction with Pawsons Road was known as the Broadway.

In Pawsons Road stood the Lord Palmerston on the corner of Palmerston Road. In 1913 the public house was sold to the Joynson Memorial Hall Baptist church, situated at the end of Pawsons Road, who also opened the Joynson Brotherhood and Institute on the pub premises.

The South Suburban Co-op had their dairy and milk depot in Farnley Road. The short gentleman on the left was Mr Slatter, who was in charge of the horses; Mr Feist was the depot manager. This view dates from 1922.

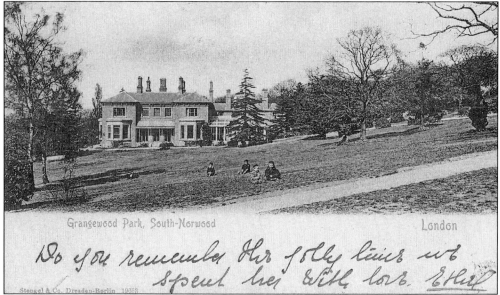

Grangewood Park, South-Norwood   London

Do you remember the jolly time we spent here? With love. Ethel

Stengel & Co. Dresden-Berlin 19055

Grangewood, originally part of the Manor of Whitehorse, was known as Whitehorse Wood and is one of a few surviving fragments of the Great North Wood. John Davidson Smith, who laid out the Beulah Spa and bought the Manor from John Cator, constructed a road from the Spa to the road junction by White Horse Farm. This formed the line of Grange Road. The wood became a private estate. The mansion was built around 1860 and after Croydon Corporation bought the estate for the public in 1900 the house became Croydon's first embryonic museum.

To complement the ornamental gardens Croydon Council established a bowling green, tennis courts and a bandstand. Band concerts entertained the public during summer months and the Thornton Heath Prize Band played there regularly. After the Second World War the mansion fell into disrepair and was demolished in 1960. The foundations were retained and laid out as formal gardens. The bandstand was also taken down.

Nine

New Thornton Heath

The ironmongery business run by George and Jack Scratchley was known as 'Scratchley's Corner' and was situated in Woodville Road at the junction with Norwich Road. The Scratchley brothers built a number of houses in the 1920s in the vicinity of the High Street and Grange Road. Brewers now occupy the building.

In 1901 a Primitive Methodist chapel was established in Woodville Road on the corner of Foulsham Road. The chapel suffered severe damage from a flying bomb in 1944. In 1950 it was sold to the Christadelphians who now occupy the hall in Foulsham Road. Flats were built on the site after 1971.

Parchmore Road widens considerably at the junction with Brigstock Road. Here was Colliers Water Green, also known as Walkers Green. This area was tidied up and made into a formal garden when the Clock Tower was erected in 1900.

The Methodist church on the corner of Fernham Road and Parchmore Road began life in 1900. After extensive internal alterations in the 1960s the original main entrance now gives access to the thriving youth and community centre while worship takes place on the upper level.

The Anglican presence in New Thornton Heath was established with the building of St Paul's church in 1872, constructed of Kentish rag and Bath stone. It was enlarged in 1901, hence the rather crooked outside appearance.

The Lord Napier pub in Beulah Road, *c.* 1908. The pub dates from the 1870s and is named after Robert Napier, who was created Baron Napier in 1868 after his daring rescue of English prisoners held in Magdala in Abyssinia (modern Ethiopia). In recent years the pub has become noted for its jazz sessions.

Beulah Road in the 1920s, with the bell tower of the school just beyond the shops on the right.

The original fire station on the corner of Beulah Road, showing the horse-drawn engine, before the fire service transferred to the new station in Brigstock Road. This was a volunteer force but the appliance was provided by Croydon Corporation who stipulated in 1885 that the rent should not exceed £15 per annum and that expenses for the horses were not to exceed £8 per year, with any further costs to be met by donations and fund-raising events. The horses were stabled at the rear of the Fountain Head public house.

The first school in Beulah Road was run by the Surrey Congregational Union, but in 1871 the premises were taken over by the Croydon School Board. By 1891 there were 1,000 pupils on the roll. The original buildings fronting Beulah Road were demolished in 1930 and the new classrooms were opened by Thomas Betteridge of the Croydon Education Committee in April 1932.

One of the classes in Beulah Road School, in the early 1920s.

Beulah Baptist church in Beulah Crescent opened in 1910. It was built as the Spurgeon Memorial church commemorating the founding of the first church, now next door, by Charles Haddon Spurgeon, the celebrated preacher. Spurgeon lived on Beulah Hill at Westwood House (now Spurgeon's College). The central area of the crescent was a nursery.

Some early cottages in Sandfield Place in 1935. They were once part of Parchmore Farm.

J. Baker's greengrocery and fishmonger business in Norbury Road. It was typical of the small corner shops that served the needs of the community in Thornton Heath and other areas.

The stone-laying ceremony of the United Methodist Free Church took place in 1880 on a site in Moffat Road on land originally purchased by David Betteridge, a local grocer, for church purposes. This postcard view taken in 1908 shows the then minister, Revd H. Buxton. Revd Willis Bryars relocated the Church to the newly built Downsview Methodist church in 1930. Fenton Court now occupies the site of the original church building.

Livingstone Road, seen here around 1920, was one of a number of roads named after noted Victorian explorers, missionaries and military leaders. In the vicinity are Mersham, Burlington, Milner, Buller and Kitchener Roads

Howberry Road in festive mood for the Coronation of King George V in 1911.

Cows in the fields opposite 88 Virginia Road in 1925, before the houses on the opposite side were built. Part of Biggin Farm, after 1870 this area became a brickfield until 1923 when building development took place. The estate is known locally as the Americas because many of the roads are named after American states.

The 84th London Company of the Boys' Brigade was originally formed at Moffatt Road United Methodist church. The company later moved with the church to Downsview Methodist church, situated at the junction of Downsview Road, Waddington Way and Virginia Road. By this time it was the 5th Company of the East Surrey Battalion Boys' Brigade, who are seen here in 1962 outside Downsview. Since 1965 the company has been known as the 5th Croydon.

Ten

War Years

General conscription during the First World War did not take place until 1916. Between the commencement of hostilities in 1914 and that date various recruitment drives took place, including a great procession through the streets of Croydon in October 1915. The procession is seen here turning out from St James's Road.

Many of the Croydon Council schools in the north of Croydon were requisitioned for use as military hospitals, providing 1,000 beds in the borough for wounded soldiers. Stanford Road School was one school converted in this way, and the hospital specialized in jaw injuries. The hospitals were closed in the spring of 1919. The school became Norbury Manor Secondary Boys' School but was demolished in March 1987 and sheltered accommodation for the elderly built on the site.

In the military hospitals, wards were created in the classrooms. For a period the nurses were members of the Australian nursing service.

Nearby Norbury Golf Course became the sports ground for those convalescing in the military hospital. The golf course was once the site of Streatham Race Course and in recent years became the sports ground of National Westminster Bank.

The calendar on the desk indicates that the photograph of the hospital secretary was taken on 19 February 1918.

Ingram Road School Military Hospital in 1917. The school itself opened in 1905, with mixed infants', juniors' and seniors' departments. In 1958 the girls transferred to a new building known as Westwood School. Three years later the juniors and infants relocated to the new David Livingstone School, leaving Ingram Road School purely as a senior boys' school.

Military personnel and patients pose for the photograph in the playground of Ingram Road School on 24 March 1917. King George V and Queen Mary paid a visit to this hospital as well as Stanford Road Military Hospital in January 1916.

The aftermath of the V1 that hit Brigstock Road on 16 July 1944. Many houses were destroyed or damaged. New flats were built on the site on the corner of Quadrant Road after the war and Trumble Gardens were laid out on the opposite side of the road.

Moffatt Road after blast damage caused by a V1. The WRVS and the Salvation Army, as seen here, did much work offering tea and refreshment from their mobile canteens as well as practical, moral and spiritual support.

Members of the 32nd Battalion (Factory) Home Guard seen here at their headquarters in West Thornton Primary School in Thornton Road.

The 62nd Surrey (Norbury) Battalion of the Home Guard had their HQ at St Christopher's School (formerly Grosvenor House) in London Road, Thornton Heath. Three members are holding for view a map of Norbury and Thornton Heath should sector Z4, in which they operated. The flats of Warwick Gardens are in the background.

Eleven

People

Alderman James Trumble, here seen at a 'Streets of Adventure' fundraising event in 1934, was a grocer whose shop was on the corner of Bensham Manor Road. Trumble Gardens in Brigstock Road, created after the V1 disaster in July 1944, were named after him. The 'Streets of Adventure' were started by the Surrey Street and Church Street Ttraders' Association to raise money for Croydon General Hospital.

HRH Princess Mary, Viscountess Lascelles, at the opening of Lodge Road clinic in Broad Green on 18 May 1926. Princess Mary was the sister of Prince Albert, later George VI.

Samuel Coleridge-Taylor, the composer, has been adopted as Croydon's own as he lived for most of his life in the Croydon area. He was born on 15 August 1875 and a year later the family moved to Croydon. His father left England shortly afterwards and his mother brought him up alone. He became a chorister at St George's Presbyterian church and later at St Mary's, Addiscombe. He spent six years at the Royal College of Music. Shortly after his marriage Coleridge-Taylor lived in Dagnall Park, South Norwood, but between 1907 and 1910 he resided at Hill Crest in London Road, Norbury, on the corner of Ederline Avenue. Coleridge-Taylor found it had drawbacks as '...all the manifold traffic of this main road from London to Brighton rattled and rumbled by with brief intermission all through the twenty-four hours.' His best known work is the *Hiawatha* trilogy. He died of pneumonia on 1 September 1912.

At the League of Nations fête in Dunheved Road on 26 June 1926 the Deputy Mayor, Alderman Southwell, is patronizing Brenda Murly's collecting tin. The Murly family lived in the London Road near Heathview Road.

The Farleys were an old Croydon farming family. Thomas Farley lived at Dovercourt and is remembered in the name of the public house in the High Street, formerly the Wilton Arms. John Farley (1825-94), his cousin, seen in this photograph, lived for a time at Brigstock House and was instrumental in providing the land for the Croydon Union Infirmary. Both Thomas and John Farley held high office in Croydon. John served on the Croydon Board of Guardians and was a councillor and alderman as well as church warden at Croydon Parish Church. John Farley died on 25 August 1894 and is buried in Queens Road cemetery.

Twelve

St Stephen's

In 1904 Revd Augustus George Edwards was appointed a Curate of St Saviour's and Priest-in-Charge of the Mission. When the parish was created in 1909 he became the first vicar, remaining in the post until his death in December 1932.

The ceremony of 'digging the first sod' prior to construction of the foundations took place on 28 March 1908 by Lady Edridge. The land on which St Stephen's church was built had been purchased from the Peacock family, who lived opposite at Grosvenor House, for £1,500.

Two months later, on 16 May 1908, Mrs Randall Davidson, wife of the Archbishop of Canterbury, laid the foundation stone. The Revd Edwards' wife is seen standing on the wheelbarrow to obtain a better view!

Members of the congregation were invited to buy and lay bricks. The girl in the centre is Doris Godfrey. Mrs Godfrey is standing to her left.

Clearly a happy day, judging by everyone's smiling faces.

Construction of the church building took place throughout 1908. The architect was William Samuel Weatherley (1851-1922). He was a pupil of Sir George Gilbert Scott. Weatherley's church restorations included Brandesburton in Yorkshire, Soundby near Gainsborough and Shere church in Surrey. He also had a successful practice in Holland, where Twente church is based on his designs for St Stephen's. Note the horse behind the pile of timber.

Choir and dignitaries processing down Winterbourne Road from the mission church to the stone-laying ceremony of the new church. Note the granite setts forming a crossing over the road. In the days when roads were muddy in winter and dusty in summer, the crossing would be nt by cleaners to ensure the hems of ladies' dresses would not get dirty.

Another procession in Warwick Road, this time on the occasion of the laying of the cornerstone.

Mary Anne Edwards, aunt of the vicar, laid the cornerstone on 21 September 1912.

St Stephen's church decorated with flags and bunting for the cornerstone ceremony. The first houses in Strathyre Avenue can be seen to the right. The trees in the distance were felled in 1926 to make way for the row of shops known as Warwick Parade on the London Road.

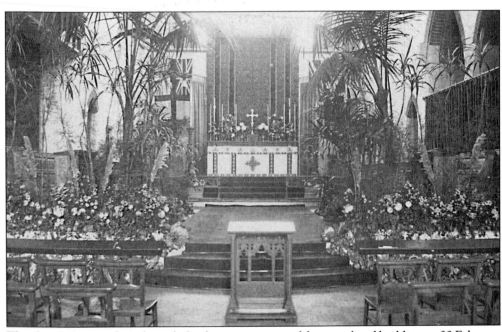

The church decorated inside ready for the consecration of the completed building on 22 February ˀ14 by the Archbishop of Canterbury, Randall Davidson. The foundations for a tower and the ˀings of tower steps were formed but th tower itself never constructed.